I0436617

Digits to Dollar

A Blueprint for Building a Profitable
Home-Based Bookkeeping Business

Marvin Brown

TABLE OF CONTENT

INTRODUCTION

Are you seeking for ways to earn some more money since you're sick of living paycheck to paycheck? You're in luck, though! It's never been simpler to make money online, and in the next section, we'll teach you how to set up a profitable online accounting service.

This guide will provide you with the necessary tools to transform your love of numbers into a successful online business, regardless of whether you're a professional bookkeeper or just trying to acquire the skills.

Does working from home and making money seem like your idea of heaven?

In January 2019, an increasing number of American workers began working remotely. Opportunities for freelance employment and remote work have greatly expanded.

Benefits of working from home are numerous. These consist of the ability to work from any location and having a flexible schedule. You may even work from a beach or your favorite lunch location. The nice thing is that you can still work full-time.

Writing logical sentences and improving your grammar are prerequisites for many remote jobs, including content creation, editing, and proofreading. Don't worry if you're not very skilled at writing. Some jobs don't require writing skills, such as remote bookkeeping.

Tracking a company's financial records is the primary responsibility of a remote bookkeeper. Anybody can pursue a career in this field, even if they don't have any experience or a public accounting qualification.

It's not as difficult to launch a virtual bookkeeping company as it seems. To begin learning how to set up your virtual bookkeeping services firm, use this step-by-step simple guide.

The potential to excel as a virtual accountant has few bounds. To get started, you don't need a business degree, a ton of cash, or previous expertise in the industry. To earn additional money from home, all you need is the will to do so.

You may be reading because you've been searching for home business ideas. Alternatively, you might want to know that the job you do counts.

You're interested in learning how to launch a virtual bookkeeping business?

Everything you require to launch an online bookkeeping services business will be covered in this guide, along with much more.

CHAPTER ONE

Important Details About Online Bookkeeping Services

Here are some essential details regarding remote bookkeeping positions.

There is no need for a license or certification. Although bookkeeping qualifications are available and can aid in future business expansion, you can launch your venture and make a respectable living without one. Certification is something you may always pursue when you have a steady job.

A degree in finance, economics, or accounting is not required. Although not required, these degrees can help you stand out from the competition and attract more clients. You can start an accounting job without any prior experience or formal education in the field.

You'll start off making between $12 and $15 per hour if you have no experience. But it is extremely possible to earn more than $30 per hour in a few years. Specialists can command over $60 an hour.

Numerous possibilities exist for remote, freelance, and part-time virtual bookkeeping. Opportunities for all three may be found on networking websites like LinkedIn and employment platforms like FlexJobs. Numerous companies are looking for freelance bookkeepers on freelancing marketplaces like Upwork.

This task is highly-scalable. Most bookkeepers start solo, managing client work alone. Eventually, you may accrue enough clients to make it worthwhile to launch a bookkeeping business and employ staff members. You can serve more (and larger) clients and make more money in less time if you do this.

The Skills You Require

The following skills are necessary for success as a bookkeeper.

1. Proficiency with at least one bookkeeping application, such Intuit's QuickBooks or Xero.

2. **Sharp basic math skills**: Although you won't be studying advanced calculus, you should be comfortable working with numbers and have the ability to spot irregularities.

3. Addressing issues: It's your responsibility to find the error's cause and figure out how to fix it if anything doesn't look right.

4. Excellent client service and communication: Bookkeepers frequently deal with invoices and payments and must communicate with suppliers and consumers.

5. Organization: Taxes, the fiscal year's conclusion, monthly/quarterly financial statements, and other deadlines will all need to be balanced.

6. Business abilities: If you work as a freelance bookkeeper, you'll need to be proficient in client communication, pricing your services, marketing yourself to potential customers, and bookkeeping for your own company.

What Does a Freelance Bookkeeper Do?

A bookkeeper is a person who helps a business manage and keep track of its finances. They usually supervise sales, spending, and the creation of financial reports. Virtual bookkeepers don't need to be physically present in an office; they can operate from home. The fact that all bookkeeping activities may be completed online or using computer software makes this configuration attractive.

Depending on your chosen company model, you may choose to work for one customer or several if you decide to do freelance accounting.

Although it sounds like an exciting job, keeping dozens of books safe from damage is not the nature of bookkeeping. In actuality, bookkeeping entails managing small firms' daily expenses.

Online bookkeepers handle a variety of tasks, including managing budgets, creating financial reports, handling invoices, managing cash flow, tracking sales, producing statements, reconciling bank statements, and recording financial transactions. Because bookkeepers may work remotely from any location, the online component arises from this feature of the job.

Making financial statements, keeping track of invoices, documenting financial transactions, filing payroll, monitoring sales, and maintaining financial records are some of the tasks you could be asked to complete. Put differently, you'll have the freedom to embrace your inner "number nerd."

Unless you specialize, you'll work with a variety of customers in different sectors as a freelance bookkeeper. What's the finest thing, then? A college degree or prior accounting expertise are not prerequisites.

What's the Difference Between a Bookkeeper and an Accountant?

Making the distinction between bookkeepers and accountants is essential. Both are essential in helping business owners, but accountants need a bachelor's degree in addition to frequently obtaining other certificates. Accountants offer insights and financial analysis.

However, bookkeepers are not required to have any formal schooling or a particular degree. Many people can work in online bookkeeping since skills like using spreadsheets and specialized software can be learnt on their own.

Kinds of Jobs for Remote Bookkeepers

There are two primary types of online bookkeeping opportunities:

1. Part-time jobs

2. Freelance work

Each has benefits and drawbacks.

Jobs for Part-Time Online Bookkeepers

You work as a W2 employee for one firm in a part-time online bookkeeping position, receiving a set hourly wage and a consistent flow of work.

Many of these jobs are offered by online bookkeeping companies. On the other hand, you can also work for a non-bookkeeping company as an internal remote bookkeeper.

For instance, you may be employed remotely by an online store as a bookkeeper.

Freelance Bookkeeping Jobs

Although you will have to find your own clients, freelance bookkeeping jobs provide greater freedom since you may determine your own timetable.

It could be worth your time and effort to do this. You might opt to focus on particular services or sectors as a freelancer in order to build your expertise in one or more domains. Better long-term scalability and far bigger earnings may result from this.

What is the Potential Income for a Remote Bookkeeper?

In the US, remote bookkeepers earn around $48,691 annually. Additionally, as your virtual bookkeeping business expands and you gain more expertise, you might make up to $63,500 annually.

Beginner Bookkeeper Salary

In their first year, freelance bookkeepers often make between $14.66 and $23 per hour, which adds up to a significant $30,500 to $48,691 yearly (and more with experience).

First-year earnings will also be less than in subsequent years because of start-up costs for things like business cards, office supplies, accounting software, and course subscriptions (more on this later).

For your new bookkeeping venture, you'll also need to create a website. Although it seems like a difficult undertaking, it's actually more easier than you may expect!

Experienced Bookkeeper Salary

What precisely will you get paid after you have experience, then?

With several years of expertise, freelance bookkeepers may expect to make up to $30.53 per hour, or about $63,500 annually. Some independent bookkeepers may make more than this, particularly if they have an accounting degree or other related degree in addition to bookkeeping certificates.

Remember that you don't need a degree to succeed in this field, even if it might assist you start making more money. As long as they remain committed, build trusting relationships with future customers, and invest the time to master the requisite skills, anybody can work from home as a virtual bookkeeper and make a good career.

Your place of residence can also have an impact on your income; US cities with higher hourly wages are Lake Marcel-Stillwater, New York City, and Green River.

Utilize the familiar desktop applications by accessing it via a hosted virtual desktop.

It seems easy, doesn't it? That's true, but you might still be wondering, "How does one go about running a virtual bookkeeping business?"

This is how you respond to it:

Certain clients may require you to take care of all or most bookkeeping duties, including creating invoices, charging clients, and processing payroll. In order to pay invoices, you might even need to email copies of the invoices to the customer for approval and obtain a signature stamp.

Certain clients will do tasks at their location, such as bill entry, check writing, invoice submitting, and other tasks. In this scenario, you will be in charge of making sure they enter data correctly, obtaining financial papers, balancing bank accounts and statements, and more.

Virtual bookkeepers also provide their services for consultations on cash flow, late payments from clients, budget planning, and other financial matters.

Part of a virtual bookkeeper's duties will include recording receipts and entering data. It is your responsibility to maintain track of receipts, categorize costs, and note who and how much was paid. You are in charge of keeping track of payments and resolving any problems with invoices related to income.

But the job you do goes much beyond just entering data into a spreadsheet. Additionally, bookkeepers are in charge of creating the following four important financial statements:

Balance sheets, or a description of the clients' financial status.

Income statement, or a look at the earnings and outlays of the customer over time

A statement of retained profits, also known as a statement of changes in equity, illustrates how owners' share capital, reserves, and retained earnings fluctuate over time.

An accounting of the cash and cash equivalents coming into and going out of the business is called a cash flow statement.

What is Required to Work as an Online Bookkeeper?

The same prerequisites that apply to on-site bookkeepers should also apply to virtual bookkeepers. Plus, a laptop and dependable internet. Bookkeepers often possess strong arithmetic, accounting, and computer abilities.

Don't worry if you haven't had formal training. Numerous certification programs and classes are available for you to select from in order to advance your business and acquire new abilities.

A blog about beginning an internet bookkeeping business is Bookkeepers.com.

The Advantages of Virtual Bookkeeping

Owning your own online bookkeeping business and working from home has many benefits these days. The benefits are genuine; you can

1. Create your own timetable, so it may be as flexible as you like.

2. Begin your day at any time you want.

3. Most days, wear sweatpants.

4. Since your pay is not fixed by anyone, challenge yourself to make more money.

5. Make lunch at home.

6. Spend time with your dogs and take rests when needed.

What sounds better than that, really? Let's expand on the advantages of virtual bookkeeping now.

What are the Weekly Work Hours for Virtual Bookkeepers?

As a virtual bookkeeper, you can work as much or as little as you choose throughout a regular workweek.

You can work 20 hours a week if you'd want to work as a part-time employee for yourself.

You can work fifty hours a week if you want to be a headless chicken.

Recall that this is your own business, not an accounting position. Thus, you decide how many customers, how many hours, and how long you want to work a week.

Which Kind of Clients are Served by a Virtual Bookkeeper?

The best thing about working remotely as a bookkeeper is that you may work with nearly any kind of small business.

While accounting practices vary from nation to nation, bookkeeping is a global language that is spoken the same wherever a customer is located.

With the use of modern cloud-based technologies, you may connect with more people. Paper receipts, in-person customer meetings, and receiving papers by fax are all things of the past.

Additionally, cloud apps aid in your market positioning in a cutthroat environment. You may take on a number of administrative responsibilities, update reports, and enable clients to view their financial information on the spot.

CHAPTER THREE

The Advantages of Outsourcing Bookkeeping Services

You should be aware of your value to a small business before trying to pitch yourself to potential customers.

Experts in overseeing a company's daily financial operations are bookkeepers. They provide small business owners with essential information to help them make future financial decisions.

Any kind of organization, regardless of size, sector, or style, need bookkeeping and accounting services.

You and other outsourced bookkeepers can be more cost-effective for the business, flexible in their adaptability, and able to view things from a different angle. Payroll taxes, health insurance, 401(k), and paid time off are all covered by your employer and are not borne by your client.

Aside from the dull technical aspects, you also provide a core set of functional benefits that can have an instant positive effect on a business's financial stability.

1. You are an expert at balancing books.

On-site bookkeepers are prone to missing deadlines, being inefficient, and being inaccurate; however, this is not you.

Depending on the bookkeeping requirements of each customer, you implement specialized methods. Your clients may count on you to provide consistent and precise bookkeeping services, and to steer clear of:

- hiring and educating new employees ($)

- Using receipts improperly

- forgetting to take a recording of something

- incorrectly submitting expenses

Additionally, as their bookkeeper, fast-growing companies could look to you to handle payroll and payroll taxes. Thus, it's crucial that you make accuracy and punctuality a top priority in your company.

2. You're less expensive than an internal bookkeeper.

Companies may save a ton of time and money by using virtual bookkeeper instead of hiring an internal bookkeeper, which is one of the main advantages.

Consider examining applications; conducting interviews; recruiting and training staff; and possible employee turnover. It's possible that some companies won't want to pay for a full-time worker who is less productive than you.

3. Less interruptions, improved data, and reporting

As a bookkeeping service, you may give businesses more accurate and thorough data. You could also be more productive because you work from home, which reduces stress and other distractions.

Reports on profit and loss, trends, costs, and other topics can be provided by external bookkeepers on a daily, weekly, or monthly basis.

In order for clients to stick with you over the long term, it is important to instill confidence in them.

4. You may provide remote data access to your clients.

Giving key personnel in your client's business access to data is a component of virtual accounting.

When accounting first started out, we showed our work to customers using floppy disks, PCs, and abacuses.

These days, virtual bookkeepers use cloud-based accounting software more strategically to enable stakeholders—small company owners—to see data on mobile devices from anywhere.

The secret is to keep providing easy experiences that improve your working connection. For your strategy to stay fresh and keep your client's attention, it must be customized.

5. Increased safety

Ensuring the safety and security of your customers' financial data is a crucial responsibility, as every competent bookkeeper is aware. This entails discussing with them your priorities for security and who should have access to what information.

Are the accounting and bookkeeping records safeguarded against power outages, floods, and fires?

Does your program have a backup of its data? (Online bookkeeping programs like Xero and QuickBooks make this automatic.)

How Can Information be Prevented from Getting into the Wrong Hands?

These are the kinds of inquiries concerning data security that your clients will have. Making clients feel comfortable entrusting you with their most important business data is your aim.

Big bookkeeping business challenges

Operating a virtual bookkeeping service has its hurdles, just like launching any other business. Among the challenges you may encounter if you begin offering online bookkeeping services are:

Software purchases and updates often come with high upfront fees.

You must be tech-savvy and capable of troubleshooting basic computer issues.

Liability concerns surround inadequate records, supervision by regulators, modifications to the law, and other matters.

Data belonging to your clients must be protected in a safe, encrypted environment.

CHAPTER FOUR

Starting a Virtual Bookkeeping Business Step-by-Step.

You are an important part of other people's businesses' operations and success as bookkeepers. Establishing your own bookkeeping business requires careful planning from the beginning.

Future clients will see you as professional if you have a well-organized workspace. Additionally, it will free you up to concentrate on bookkeeping, your favorite job, rather than fixing problems with the base of your business's operations.

The encouraging good news? Getting started doesn't have to be tough. The process of starting a bookkeeping business might be intimidating due to the variety of approaches available. I've distilled the procedure down into manageable phases based on my personal experience starting a business of my own and my in-depth study on the topic of accounting business setup.

Not as horrible as you had imagined? We'll go into detail about each topic and why it's critical to the success of your accounting business in the phases that follow.

1. Being Aware of the Need for Virtual Bookkeeping Services

Determining the market for the services you want to provide is one of the first stages in launching a virtual bookkeeping service. A growing number of companies are shifting their activities, including financial administration, online in the current digital era. As more businesses attempt to outsource their bookkeeping requirements in order to save time and money, this has resulted in a rise in demand for virtual bookkeeping services.

The growth of the gig economy and the rise in small enterprises and entrepreneurship are key factors boosting the need for virtual bookkeeping services. These people frequently go to virtual bookkeepers for help since they lack the means or knowledge to manage their own bookkeeping.

Furthermore, the need for virtual financial services has increased along with the rise in remote work and flexible work schedules. It's simpler for you to collaborate with your clients from anywhere in the globe because companies are searching for remote-ready virtual bookkeepers.

Not to mention, the COVID-19 epidemic has sped up the transition to remote and digital work, which has raised demand for virtual bookkeeping services even more.

You can write a more focused and successful business strategy and sell your services to potential customers more effectively if you are aware of the need for virtual bookkeeping services.

2. Get Certification

For people who love numbers—that is, the "working with big numbers" and "earning big numbers" sorts of love—virtual bookkeeping is the perfect career path. Formal experience is not required, however in order to learn the ins and outs of the business, we highly advise enrolling in a course taught by professionals in the field.

To draw in clients, you must, nonetheless, brush up on your numeracy abilities, master bookkeeping software, and develop your marketing talents.

Certain abilities, including organization, comprehending numbers, and attention to detail, are required; they may be learned through online courses.

Although certification isn't strictly necessary to get started, it does demonstrate to your clients that you are qualified to handle their finances. Plus, having the information required for the position can boost your confidence. There are two options for obtaining training: at a community college or through an organization.

Since the government does not control bookkeeping credentials, it is crucial to obtain your certification from a reputable institution. The American Institute of Professional Bookkeepers (AIPB) and the National Association of Certified Public Bookkeepers (NACPB) are the top two. Both provide tests and courses covering every aspect of bookkeeping.

We have the solution to your question, "What kind of capital do I need to start a virtual bookkeeping business?"

If you currently own a laptop, you'll need at least $1,000 to get started. This might include the cost of a DIY website and a QuickBooks software subscription. Monthly plans start at $20.

Remember to set aside some more funds as a safety net throughout the early going.

5. Draft a strategy of business.

You'll need to create a business strategy to determine how you'll get paid as a virtual bookkeeper.

Before launching the business, it is imperative that everyone draft a business plan.

A minimum of what your business strategy ought to contain is:

Market research on your industry, rivals, and target customers

An examination of your advantages, disadvantages, opportunities, and dangers

Do some research on the issue you assist clients in solving.

How your service solves the problem at a reasonable cost

Your current financial situation, anticipated cash flow, costs, and earnings (after all, you work as a bookkeeper!)

How you want to expand the business

Your advertising plans

6. Name and Structure of the Business

Selecting the right kind of business entity is a crucial decision made at the outset of every venture. In the United States, there are four typical structures to pick from:

- Sole proprietorship (Schedule C)
- Partnership
- Company with Limited Liability (LLC)
- Corporation

If you are starting something fresh with little capital, you may want to think about becoming a single owner.

Nevertheless, BEWARE AND SPEAK WITH AN ATTORNEY BEFORE YOU START YOUR BUSINESS.

As businesses expand, a lot of bookkeepers—as well as small proprietors of service-based businesses, for that matter—move into LLCs. Your choice of business entity structure affects both your tax obligations and your personal liabilities in the event that your company is sued.

It's time to register your business with your state once you've decided on its name and organizational structure.

Knowing what you need to be in business is the first step. To begin, review the laws of your state and municipality. To register for an LLC and obtain an EIN for your company, many states might need you to have a business license.

Getting a fantastic business banking account is one thing you shouldn't overlook. For any online accounting firm, Azlo provides a free online business checking account. Opening an account just takes a few minutes, and you can plan transfers, make payments, and deposit checks from anywhere.

7. Organize your hardware.

A lot of virtual bookkeepers make additional hardware investments. And for good reason: You get more freedom and a competitive edge when you own a dependable laptop that utilizes cloud technologies. Keep in mind that you will depend on this technology on a daily basis.

The majority of software is compatible with both PCs and Macs, so the kind of computer you select is a matter of taste.

Whether you want to work on a desktop computer or a laptop is one thing to think about. For example, a laptop would be a better option if you're providing bookkeeping services while touring the world.

In any case, purchasing a larger screen is a smart move to lessen eye strain. Staring at an 11- or 13-inch screen all day long can easily cause eye fatigue.

8. Expanding Your Customer Base

When looking for freelance bookkeeping possibilities, it might be helpful to understand the work from the perspective of a bookkeeper. During an interview, a qualified bookkeeper provided the following description of the position:

"Consider bookkeeping as the high-tech equivalent of managing your home's finances." Every company must keep track of every dollar coming in and going out. This is simple in principle, but it's not in reality. Bookkeepers provide precise financial data to business owners, enabling them to delegate financial chores and concentrate on their areas of competence.

After establishing your virtual bookkeeping business and obtaining the required tools, the following stage is to begin attracting clients. Combining price, marketing, and networking tactics can help achieve this.

Establishing a network is crucial to growing your client base. This might involve interacting with local businesses, joining groups for professionals, or going to industry events. You may obtain useful contacts and business-growing recommendations by establishing ties with other experts in your industry.

Another crucial component of expanding your client base is marketing. This might involve putting together and distributing marketing materials, building a website, or advertising your services on social networking sites. You may expand your clientele and reach a larger audience by efficiently promoting your services.

Pricing is also a significant component in building your client base. Finding out the going pricing for virtual bookkeeping services in your community requires market research. When determining your charges, you should also take into account the time and effort needed for each customer as well as your personal costs.

It's crucial to keep in mind that developing your client base requires time and work, but you may establish your company and draw in long-term customers by persistently contacting prospective customers, offering top-notch service, and charging a reasonable price.

9. Create a branded email address and website.

Having a polished, business-like website and branded email address is a smart idea before you start attracting clients.

An intuitive website that showcases your expertise and the bookkeeping services you provide should be the aim.

It should be simple for a potential customer to get in touch with you over the phone or via email while they browse your website.

Website builders: It's not necessary for your website to be expensive.

To quickly construct a stunning website, use a website builder such as Squarespace. Alternatively, you may create a more personalized website by using WordPress.

There's a slight learning curve with WordPress, but once you get the hang of it, you can convert your business site into anything you want.

Of course, you may always pay a firm to build one for you if you have the money.

SavvySites, for instance, offers personalized websites for businesses. They are bookkeepers only, and they can construct a website with your material, photos, and logo.

Business email.

It is more probable that prospective clients would want to collaborate with you if you appear more professional on the internet.

Your virtual bookkeeping business will appear professional if you choose a business email address that incorporates your name and your company domain (yourbusiness.com). It's an affordable method of demonstrating honesty and dependability.

This is the simplest method, while there are other methods to obtain a branded email account.

Purchase a domain name for yourself (from DreamHost or GoDaddy). Include it in your G Suite account for just $6 a month, get a business email address.

G Suite also includes access to G Docs, Sheets, Slides, and other office applications, as well as 30GB of cloud storage and shared calendars.

This facilitates the organization, security, and backup of client files on a cloud that you may access from any location.

10. Software for bookkeeping services

In addition, you'll want a respectable tech stack. Start with the following three virtual bookkeeper resources:

Select a trustworthy bookkeeping software for your company.

You may better manage the workflow and remain on top of your clients' bookkeeping with the aid of reliable software. Your clients will appreciate you if you put in place the appropriate resources and assistance since it makes a great difference.

The top three programs for virtual bookkeepers, according to Fundera, are:

- Xero
- QuickBooks
- Sage One

Providing dependable, cloud-based software to clients facilitates the bookkeeping process.

You may log in to ensure they make correct entries, reconcile bank and account balances, recover statements, and more without the need for a paper trail.

Programs like as QuickBooks also provide training so your customer may become proficient with it and feel at ease using it.

If you wish to handle your clients' funds more skillfully, you could also want to employ tools like budgeting, invoicing, and financial planning software. These technologies can offer useful insights into your clients' financial situation in addition to automating tedious processes like creating invoices and keeping track of spending.

Purchase a platform for video conferences.

Using a video conference is preferable than texting or making phone calls while conducting interviews or client meetings.

Why? Because in-person conversations make both parties seem more human. It also enables you get to know them better and operate in a more intimate, intuitive type of approach.

Online meetings are made simple by these three programs, all of which offer a free version:

One of the things you should learn about if you want to launch a virtual bookkeeping company is marketing. To make sure your business is seen and has a shot at generating leads, employ these promotion strategies.

Create a website that is mobile-friendly.

Making your website mobile-friendly is one easy approach to market your bookkeeping services.

If your page loads slowly, mobile consumers are more inclined to visit a competitor's website.

Moreover, data indicates that 73% of mobile devices prompt further action, and that having an optimized mobile website improves your Google search engine ranking. The key to drawing in the appropriate customers is having an organized website.

Talk on podcasts

It is impossible for small business owners to judge your credibility. An even better method to demonstrate your knowledge than hosting a podcast. It's a good idea to get on board now that the number of active podcast listeners in the US is rising.

Visit some of the most well-known industry podcasts on iTunes to see whether you'd be a good match, then send the presenter a suggestion or two. Try these fantastic accounting podcasts:

- Accounting Best Practices
- Accounting Play
- I Love Bookkeeping
- The Xero Gravity
- The Beancounter
- ACCA Podcast
- THRIVEAL Podcasts
- Cloud Stories
- College Info Geek

Provide 60-minute consults for free.

Building a connection with potential clients through consultations is quite simple, and these clients frequently become paying ones. You don't need to hire a marketer to publish the deal on your website and social media accounts; you can do it yourself with ease.

Obtain testimonials from previous customers

By showcasing testimonials, you demonstrate to prospective customers that your offerings may also have an influence on their business. Because customers can see the successes you've achieved for other companies, it speeds up the closing process.

Request a sincere testimonial about your freelance bookkeeping services from any previous employers or clients by email or text.

Use the appropriate channels for marketing

Social media self-promotion is a fantastic method of increasing visibility. All you need to do is exercise caution in your approach.

You may start on the channel that your audience spends the most time on once you know who they are. Facebook can be the ideal platform, for instance, if you provide family or individual accounting services. LinkedIn could be a better option if you exclusively work with small company owners.

Make sure your social media page is solely dedicated to providing advice and information about bookkeeping if you plan to sell there. Complete every field in your social media bio as well. It enables prospective clients to obtain from you all the information they want.

6. Register as a bookkeeper on freelance websites.

Check out freelancing websites that assist companies in finding independent bookkeepers and accountants before you spend any money on advertising. Most don't charge you to create a profile, but after you book a gig and are paid, they will collect a modest fee.

Among the best places to look for remote, independent bookkeepers are:

- Upwork offers a variety of bookkeeping jobs.
- Flexjobs for bookkeepers who want flexible schedules
- For remote bookkeeping and accounting assignments, use Freelancer.com.
- Peopleperhour for access to global clients
- Careers in entertainment for bookkeepers in the entertainment sector

Simply said, to begin looking for new bookkeeping work,

Enroll in every employment site listed above.

Complete your profile by adding a photo, experience, talents, services, costs, and other details.

Sign up to get job updates.

Publish content on trade blogs

Guest writing is an efficient method of spreading the word about your brand. To put it simply, it implies you create unique content for well-known websites inside your sector.

Visit your preferred industry blogs and check to see if they have any information on guest posting opportunities. Alternatively, you may search for "guest posts" or "contribute" plus accounting on Google to see what chances surface.

Launch a loyalty program.

Client recommendations are more likely to come your way when they are happy working with you. The best kind of advertising for virtual bookkeepers and accountants is word-of-mouth. More people trust them than sponsored social media postings or Facebook advertisements.

Start a loyalty program to get additional recommendations. You can provide your customer a gift card, discount on your services, or a charitable donation made in their honor when their referral turns into a new client. Getting referrals can bring in new business and doesn't need a lot of time or work.

Use Facebook advertisements to promote your brand.

Facebook advertising is one of the simplest methods to connect with your target market. It goes without saying that this is the most focused kind of advertising as you can target people based on their age, interest, activity, or location with videos, photos, or offers.

Which Online Resources are Helpful for Launching a Virtual Bookkeeping Business?

We've put up a shortlist of resources to assist you stay informed about everything virtual bookkeeping and accounting related and stay up to speed with industry developments. Information on publications, blogs, associations both domestically and internationally, and more is available.

While we're not advocating that you follow every accounting blog out there, it's a good idea to subscribe to a handful just to stay informed. Take a look at this list:

- Subscriptions to e-news (IRS.gov)
- Accountancy Journal
- The Insightly Accountant
- Xero Blog
- QuickBooks Blog

We don't want to brag, but if you need further assistance getting started in bookkeeping, you've come to the correct location.

Expanding and Developing Your Enterprise

You could discover that you need to scale and expand as your virtual accounting firm develops in order to meet demand. This can be adding more employees, contracting out certain work, or broadening the range of services you provide.

Taking on more employees is a terrific method to grow your company and manage a growing clientele. This may entail using virtual bookkeepers, administrative assistants, or customer support agents to respond to questions from customers.

Scaling your firm may also be accomplished through the effective outsourcing of some tasks. This might involve contracting with specialist companies or independent contractors to do duties like data entry, payroll, or financial analysis. You may concentrate on the essential elements of your company and expand it effectively with the aid of outsourcing.

Increasing the range of services, you provide is another smart strategy for growing your company. For instance, you might want to think about providing your clients with extra services like financial planning or tax preparation. This might assist you in standing out from the competition and drawing in new business.

In the end, expanding and developing your virtual accounting company will need time and work, but you can make sure that your company is set up for long-term success by putting a strong plan in place and employing the appropriate tactics.

CONCLUSION

The ability to operate remotely with customers and new cloud technologies are rapidly transforming the bookkeeping industry. Virtual bookkeepers must use it if you want to provide your company an advantage over rivals.

Never forget to concentrate on giving customers convenient and worthwhile experiences. Customers purchase from individuals, not just businesses.

Breathe deeply if all of this feels overwhelming. You may launch a successful firm by making the effort to comprehend what virtual accounting is and how it operates.

In summary, jobs as an online bookkeeper provide a steady opportunity to work from home and earn a salary above average.

Even if you have no prior expertise, remote bookkeeping gives you the chance to start a new profession and earn money from home. Bookkeepers are constantly needed by businesses, but the supply of qualified candidates for the position is never sufficient.

Bookkeeping might be a great remote career for you if you love working with numbers and solving problems, are organized, and are proficient with software.